# stretchers

*Also by Jeff Hilson:*

A Grasses Primer (Form Books, 2000)
The As (Canary Woof Press, 2000)
Tracey Traces (Kater Murr's Press, 2002)

Jeff Hilson

# stretchers

REALITY STREET
2006

Published by
Reality Street Editions
63 All Saints Street, Hastings, East Sussex TN34 3BN
**www.realitystreet.co.uk**


Typesetting & book design by Ken Edwards

Printed and bound by CPI Antony Rowe, Eastbourne

A catalogue record for this book is available from the British Library

ISBN: 1-874400-34-2

*Acknowledgements*
These poems have previously appeared as *stretchers 1-12* (Writers Forum, 2001) and *stretchers 13-33* (Writers Forum, 2002), and also in *CCCP Review, Great Works, Painted, spoken, Poetry Summit, Quid* and *The Radiator.*

*for Cheryl*

## 1-12

"I live on the island where people shout 'It is they!' at the voyagers as if they knew of their coming and feared them."

…the sawing man I fear for his legs
red white red white and he has years
this road they will dig it and widen the pave
tho it is not oxford street it is said
the rich must now walk on that side too
for graffiti there's dogshit it's a kind
of writing can be scried an inventory
taken of say colour consistency and
I won't have this neighborhood
fears of a mass break-in nor pay
for inside when you can have sound
from over there (where was angry)
the phrase "phenomenological night"
and hedges such as do you know
what I mean the word hedge is new
and used everywhere by ladies like
albert ayler's music for circus and
as in hedge-school and hedge-bird
and hedge-priest as in hedge-bantler
on the right or wrong side of the
hedge takes a sheet off the hedge or
is on the hedge regardless of others
the hedge-creeper he's a creeper crept
into a hedge for the hedge-police
would catch him for his creeping and
the hedge of hawthorn was as a cloak
to hide the creeper gone aside from
the straight way the shifter and shuffler
his means of protection as in the dancers
bottom right of bosch's garden their blind
owl-headed dance buried in a tusked bud
*schal* or *schil* rind and quarrel these
briars and brambles will protect you…

…it must be calm this going on
and off the island the marshes
will never be mentioned (what's
a marsh like on the inside) as
squalls may break out that's one
and that's one but it must be calm
and there must be a wood hard
by a wood for calm a wood built
(what will this wood do) for use
it's green for use the colour green
it must be calm the colour green
it must be seen from say up there
(what's the evidence for "please")
where there's music and could
the king hear the kept king hear
the reedy organ its mechanics its
(though he did not go ten times to
an alehouse though he too could
see) the wood the trees he was
not attached to wise men nor
wizards no this was in another
wood or forest of this and forest
of that where blue and green would
not be seen as it was on the down
said to be said to be the oldest
in playing order and now it's
hurst or horst  they have become
immobile oh see the red squirrel
ah look the nightjar oh see the red
squirrel it has the nightjar oh hear
the nightjar oh look the nightjar
oh it must be calm again…

...the disaster is necessary and known
by some by many never mind looking
for the thrill of it all three cheers for
a birth a lovely story of how to live
with how the snakes (tree snake)
shit and piss its just all fall down
up here in the trees of course I
prefer to live in a tree a leafy house
wall (you can use a leaf for to eat
to hide to wipe and to kill also they
are a poultice for fangs) can you
say keep rolling these days about
time about put them back also
put it there and you have
the one about see how they run
to the *helicalpter* but slow it down
show it slowmo (the *helicalpter* also
has been seen before) see how they
run splishy-splashy to make it last
these moments to cherish (you
should have all tape it) how slow
they splishy-splashy to the *helicalpter*
could be first people (this might
contradict against trees oh no this
might also be very bad thoughts)
yes they idle hideous sloth and now
give thanks to come to my sofa
all fall down in the *helicalpter*
you have been rescued cue you
have not been rescued you have
been delivered you have not been
saved but it has been exquisite
thank you cannot thank you enough...

…a man in a suit announces himself
takes up the doorframe and watch
the absinthe say the barman for
it makes the heart grow big and
watch it says the suit a venture
I realise and so the absinthe is
in hand to knock him about the joints
head shoulders knees and toes knees
and toes and hands arms and wrists
and the neck the nape of the neck
well it's someone I know
the green knight nape bone's
honour's gone and connected to
the scrape bone belongs to jesus
he will never go down in these
weeds today what hairy knees and
no ancestors for the crude count
merrily feinted (he never seen the
blue and green had not the interest)
in *oblige* knock knock isabel king
the poet lived tramping danger
in the shape of some and many
far to the left all the land of ever
and anon much better already
was no potent and no points the
nape bone's connected to the head
stone dictionary of the morning
sir this of that choose peggy sue
in lubbock texarcana (crew cut in
decatur sounds like "ear tug")
decatur's connected *up to the*
*'taters* see you later mister
shing-a-ling…

…will it take notes this peoples
palace name a C20th american
poet (silence) who likes poems
about barbers (hurrah) well cut
my throat there's nothing from
the longhouse here and please
save me your shit-pickings in
your all read cawl and kepi now
that's what I call related oh
look at the gleaners (they are poor
and live in france) arise arise for
hickory practice machinery will
in for a kill in for a green bridge
become perilous to the smallest
ok name a stoker by the name of
williams and the care of how
there are a hair for physic keep
old plants pull out of huge essex
take cuttings to the market agree
to abide with them go bides with
them yes sir yes sir I *am* full of wool
and soft down go down soft down go
contrary go to the country to the
flower show smell capital acanthus
see bear's breech in the wall of
the lovely prison garden and the
queen will see your man-daughters
now that's what's called related ah
pardon mine climbing rose I didn't
promise you lady's tresses or love-
in-a-mist *this* hundred year *that's*
an offence well met with silence…

…a cut hunter is a thing of
two halves with a score here
and a score there say down
one arm and it could come
off the way he drags himself
through a pampas field (I say
where are the lines of deal)
two-shoes good as three could
be a riddle as my first is in
my winchester repeater and
now we must eat his teeth
or his smile might give out
old pennies as in round them
up in the nearest pond (what's
a manchester sailor to do
with a heart girl to a a bomb
boy) he's a leader in steals
any gory head would say
look into the carnage-shed
in caves for a tribe of cross-
swallowers (swap you mine
for a brown four) a treat is
early peas and late-flowering
defence with serif on toast
(add a dash to the noise made
by a shower of gars look up
*gars*) they was this wide and
scarry with effects I'd hend
them with this net and jag
with this queer bone like it
was paradise said lester you
can do it with a piece of fat
or with a guard…

…I am not a cat I am a model
that bite on whitebait heads
as soon as say a hairy tare is
almost hairless or old clocks is
nothing special is very inter-
esting these clean london lines
out to croydon-on-the-fringe
for the sound-at-a-distance
is in the charlie bells what's
called a dutch striker as I said
on the half-hour no need to
cross the room any room for a
diamond mine (old grubby
stones will make you see-
through) until we use brass in
housing or charlie build
a city in the sea as in wave
and wave is ten thousand per
arse a city a half-a-mil a city
a walk in jack-sandals the
goddess frig of clock-winding
she was a skeleton in a tube
a train of boy-girls moving
through gold their way is free
which tells the time by silk
wound round an arbor of
two silver bells ring it ring it
who for should I buy a little
candle for my nurse was hit
and run by a bouncing angel
so as I said I am not a cat I
am a red and a green this time
to stay the year…

…an english bond the long
and short will make a summer
havoc and so use air to take
a message up and over kerbs
"shocked air" read some lips
a flemish bond is a castle that's
out in time (val you must not
say *gong* rhymes with *card*)
or what's the use of feeling
there was a young lady back
from the front (bone her dog
give it a fella I'm sick) item
picnic idem hamper had so
many hampers like whatever
a swallow won't do smack
or silk for their childrens he
watches and watches to see
the fishes leap every one has
been nicked they were stunned
like so many hills when they
are tinged with colour give it
a name in your other verse *go
to the ant* it is a sort of floor
a signal-bell a silver margin
the way a reaper looks up I
mean they were nails by the
failing poplar rarer and rarer
eulogia for thames-pulled
calf mad for golden tom the
subject waves I'm queen of
bandy a smile for your pocket
money people round mob-like
open into a column…

…I will put my hook in joy
that dwell among plants and
hedges to be a mole in the
ground and know vallejo never
is buried (he made seeds into
a good sauce) and she follows
cold cold david give her ought
and fled a league as a wild roe
and he was gone behind the
roller step-dancing *this is not
the way* neither is this a people
because I tell you it is a lie this
vessel or the lichen on it go
over and be very high say I am
a dry tree and a scab a bright
spot with kinds of very great
burnings (please let me come
on as an oilhorn and his wife)
clean the house with a bird
or the weave-hangers will make
off with pillars and the pots
groan you are all body doctors
surely do not rent my clothes
to the queen now they made
him look like ma saying I'll
wish my curtains off I can see
passing fair or a sideshow
it's like soccer out there rover
has the ball coughs perhaps
but since I am a dog look
that I can't do set-to-sail can
do wall oh oh now jane has it
says mostly it is words…

…we are the *civil* servants
(I'm a friend you can't write
that) that's haematite on
whose legs horsey horsey
quite the compass see how
my garboard strakes with a
common or plot and it's quite
massive and hackly like all
in rows you laid me out to
dry that is a sermon that is
been in a cab I saw it worn
out by spitting and tumours
(three to one it's a talent)
am orderly and not actually
rude am so gone over with
lines or misuse of drusy or
*you will get a bolt* I should
not get a heart stuck in the
river with a ten foot smile
and ribbons my how it has
become a habit to grow great
and green but read on some
way out by the chapel royal
(these use handy little biscuits
to add more windows all over
wandsworth) like gaul is now
used would rather this than
let us rim in certain stores or
can join men and branches
you can of course this could
be such a scheme that is if
this is very likely but with
I *believe* you need to…

…when we are dead (if when)
as simple and smal passed
through london (friends on the
sea-coast) we set forward some
times and rode and stopped
the thing on the street he was
a stranger and vague of the same
name something to do with
shape-like-holes the grave the
sweet pie and a piece of cheese
I am the devil I was the devil
(he got coin singing and dancing)
fish-wide where it hurts like
the man with the weed lost as I
look cram *shine* into this thing
down the road down and hooks
but it was dusty (called success)
sun rise and set the great slide
useless dozens of horses and it
was only day but he never got a
hang its field day now and shiny
buttons who had no job *I know*
*as I have lived* and people is
plain happier for lack of tread
even in broad daylight and
comfy in the sun and had no govt
did it all became a jack a roving
torch a spy-around-the-town
with the uglies and collapsing
some of that last kind feel all in
you are dead in bed with hands
to want a little house come over
to the wall this is a wall…

…men that are safe them
men them trees you have
a man's tung and niples is
as mild as may as die for a
phrase *my little blurt* "you
are enhanced" sweet fern
in a church way the salmon
(a salmon is a slithery flat
fish) one is a song is the sink
no truly they are all as still
as other men but not always
gentle come into his eyes
rare golden dots broke off
free and round sometimes
and sometimes it was shot
off pieces of fire and different
call him mister-and-ill of
444 addresses and larded
prose (in the key of *hind* and
hart-of-ten) carry summer
always carry one mind you
set out in one a man can go
'boil over' pot called a little
place a wilder lane of yellow
aspidistra (use as a shiel for
breathing simple sounds of
invasion so follow with contact
and a spike as in air in after)
rise up and so become tall as
smoke (stop) as merest nobody
as merd as boundaries the I-
do-well to carry something
over to carry off…

## 13-33

"s t r e t c h i n g

g o n e – o n – t o –"

*Maggie O'Sullivan, "Winter Ceremony"*

…silent and holy all is all is
a new harley start cold out
court court and corner bring
in green and grove to north
fields release slow hounds
sudbury hill way lope to the
over common as must-see
turns pastoral as curls ought
(thing is she is now up up &
west) *happy* you *year* turns
mass angry etc ask anyone
not not on a roundabout or
on a list so it lies bright &
thick as a pound put you
right off second life (one
I already did starring one
who goes over the twelfth)
& with venus in clouds can't
see naked spiker twinkle no
more than a hundred million
miles off (memory) a wren
ran under it *jingle jingle* all
the way home hang under it
holly shouting there it go
there in the bank (again
wrong) how it go that way
some time blood that is if
dresses over it look like
a tiny two week star who
can do with love blowed
over number whatever no
leave it simple as abc…

…am not a wolf am a word
whose faults are as *ff* written
by a fifth blonde jogger says
it all goes on under the bridge
(with my long stave I shot jill
ran to a dapple-deer) and in a
world in which you are lost
your fags *see his eyes there*
slide in and out there starring
jill cook-and-bake and two
village idiots washed her and
dressed her and and doggy
and cat were twins when they
got back (got off got on six
and six makes were just the
same have some glee *ain't*
*got no sense knots* nor as it's
a bird *and* a cake got a (like
this) 'little' house of glee as
it's a orrery as I stole inside
it was shades glided by cold
and wondrous as a slice of
heaven and honeyman gone
at 33 (see also him fiddle his
hymn to a towel) from what
a load of dripping and rhymes
this is your birth-day bee and
roses came and downward
tips no there's none nor keys
a bunch of daffs (louder)
a tidy sum tossed his forty-
five into the ripple (echo)
this is not a circular…

…bird to dawn as fox
takes child in two (king
as singer or singer smokes
a fat hair) says a tache
is a task part worker part
pasta wreck oh I am dishy
see how I am the special
our daily order is a beef
with stella stella is meltdown
stella is good morning and
an only voice she is just
an oasis please select the
electric stick for first fun
and mark it as one place
(overheard *you are a small
white*) and please rescue
from the sweetness seen
to in a field of *hands up*
if this is a time of year
and if it can not long be
held I have gone a way
from the story when every
one was at dinner and look
the ground is for digging
bye and bye (two shots)
and now we are down look
at her char and three paces
she thinks maida vale but
is far wrong three to four
tries cut and cut the catch
obligatory hair and body
a make-you-believe style
call call eve call anytime…

…once there had a little
invader come in on a jap
sandwich the filthy clammy
hand & enemy starling (a
climbing species away from
its place) & such razor feet
it was cancelled & named
as fallow land the *clowe
gilofre* sowed and lied
down in a field of shoddy
which plied with stick &
goldboots (slow frucht eater
at its head stamping ores
& flashy songs of pink
death (one two startle my
shoe-count it go up to three
o three & pick up sleepers
as had the day-sweats of
a button boy (wood stone
wood *long raised brick*
& a butylene of confused
sound used as bait like
*wretch-manoeuvres* (ah
debbie-bliss moves into
extra time) tell how to
fast on fastens eve by
coughing & weakness
now he gone a-groping
mister suck-person rays
from the first of the mouth
make it stick up on a heap
'e said fell so sick 'e did
close down the countree…

…fun *is not the only* fun
as you are too fit for the
economy (gran hit bully
with duck) answer *none*
what are the 7 kinds of shit
I want (see) & found I am
(no look) had no stars in
secret and gave advice on
& on destruction of snipe
forest (little areas of hard
froth and specks like the
hurts we get (the heart) take
the wife whenever she comes
in the margin she says this
she says I need longer words
than the words I am sighing
seem to be finger-singing
*don't fit in the waves* of bees
and honey as landscape
invasion but you had a
(how do you like it) hand in
finger-ends as lying-positions
& the main stress is can I
watch such a shine as cover
for doing it with your teeth
& (the missing pieces) mine
open hand was quite open
& the clews mean *I am gone*
*through* & I compare you
to a smew (sudden & often)
which come from a rumour
of daddy took it away…

…we in the middle did do
it cut his house down for
hack of night cut cut and
with fly and buzz-hammer
took out the heart of it out
side laid it round town in a
bush everywhere a garden
it was old time and did with
feeling how it was a fine
spread so then it rained for
him over his pieces of home
and for he said you cunt
with love (what's 't' for its)
high time I would not fight
had he'd a had a hirondelle
(which is a case of same old
for leaf) and so around and
more around like what are you
writing in what nice place
(this is gb he is fawn and in
charge) this his coney after
fighting these his next heads
and admired the complex city
breaks to wit the district
zone of rio also ripped time
the awk time of day for post
cards and talk about circles
better to say simply a hundred
fat rich men carve and shape
pass the sphere hack off all
corners go to work with a
large block in his head…

…smile your in candid trench
so shoot me I've some blonde
bombs out as doubles (every
good girl deserve a red buzzing
heart) and your it ling-boy who
fingered his walnut for sunny
delight (who did holly blue
unfurl) it was genius gimme
pink for two-up & change of
show wherein cotton & thistles
*this way for cotton & thistles*
& lips are high speed glossers
in which things are heaped
back (pull yourself & get it
in the glory hole (all he had
said slipt into the *hysteron*
*proteron* or the level of bush
as love point (a receiver is
once half way) & a cleat is
the last one in is a thistle
that time at that time a name
for these lips as slow small
glisters (curves traced out to
slide between & later) & so
hop hop has lost his lean his
wife could eat no floaters
also the right to cheap flicks
& sounds of splashing off
sallys night feathers & vowel
variants all frail peel them
like each other with our pen-
tricks move along or you
will lose it with that zee…

…I am a nurse the room my
ward piled up the "stretchers"
cap of pink and blue cut up
the men to hen (hen looks like
hen of company d) poor company
d they take alarm just being
condensed (he drips as if he
hardly gone) my ward he drips
and almost pours he looks
like steam whose chevrons
went we meanwhile filled in
greasy beef a mammoth sort
just being condensed the cots
with handles (knives and forks)
this room is filled with knives
and forks (but they both have
the loaded cups) the surgeons
have this terrible wheel can
make things vapor in this room
(though in the room the non-
coms smoke) we meanwhile
sort just being condensed hen
looks like hen though pink
and blue cut up the tin cups
of the men (both have this cap
of cut up things half-bed half-
bier the men to hen had hardly
gone) the surgeons call the golden
hours *light-heartedness* but I
a nurse am counterfeit not great
at all the "stretchers" being
condensed just piled up…

…a word is not a crystal
is a two way shoe is used
for accidents in factories
you say titty-fuck (return)
your pair of beaver hoops
& fur forms you only need
one *lights out brand* (pensi
fit into a small space and
have length and width are
used for *bell rescue* who
want low mink hangers &
lightning hands I could of
dreamed of eg cut & peel
the 1 inch limbs can you
say titty-fuck (return) who
make reading this slings &
or in corners or on carpets
fur will dry royal that slide
you fat between the manual
both sides fits all & I like
the wemen & the men &
I like you my favrite story
was pierre (no definition
found for *kinder guard* or
all four feet that run) I use
to want low mink hangers
& bridal safety (runners in
white wanted for beaver
patterns on different carpet
who make reading this say
titty-fuck or ball tong ring
tong sell to us the rest you
only need one …

…a bird with no name it
go pink pink but in some
month of may it seems
my I'm falling apart (is
the glue that holds the
funny sides the big ones
the little ones for me it
seems the other side was
busted) my tissues my
tissues would say I'm fine
otherwise I'm fine and
double jointed too and
otherwise I'm fine and
things connected with it
(long streaks of bad by
the sea shore called also
something in a garbled
form *like tell that to the*
*marines* in the summer
time like sing about a
pocketful of ruth (isn't
there tests to tell you all
the *easy marks* how the
eyes will glidder and
scatter how these birds
are disguised as wood
as devices for changing
direction (then they'll
say he's a constantly
hanging (how he's a
simple goner (now he's
almost wanted (how he
don't amount to much
(now it's june…

...his way is mirror miroir
all broke up for parade in
being a poet shame shame
& made them cry *facial action*
short phrasal spasms over
agent scully (she invades
this world only when I burst)
& frank singing pea-trees
in the fountain (he is post-op
& delivers first day cover)
drip drip goes the word-
hoard a days work for bunty
& close-ups this morning
with a quick loose pair their
perfect nerves all springing
out to play (she stabbed
the eyes on her (a comedy
of lean and favour has an
opening-closing small *i*
& a man of nonce-words
(her objet-trove her mary-
bones-a-wander his head
on her spread-about-the
hills her out-and-out) &
cut to *which it is what it is*
(your o-rings) flesh they
been and went *ars longa*
(you must buy it its by clark)
& lost her scoop-neck
to a coppermaker going
to creamery fayre & then
wonder how come it come
so easy off the tongue...

…do re mi in pup tents bill
sang notes on tap so known
I saw him sway o wise bill
smith the average man with
marks which whisperin bill
(the barroom floor the shout)
where's bill smith is in pup
tents packed and moved stuff
shirt and dirt I saw him sway
bill grinnin for you see and
left his body livin (apres dejeuner
went swimmin) (do re mi in
each fourth line a simple
cipher crumbly concrete
beams and rafters and a
roof of red tiles) hired old
hay wagon and went to do
re mi done moved again in
pup tents where we saw french
movies where a statue stood
in each fourth line a battered
statue where's bill smith and
bill he touched the keys
(a lull a barn an oft-told tale)
an old french barn and angles
giving joan where english
tourists saw french movies
diary a) she had her vision
diary b) fine trip all told and
do re mi in pup tents bill
barn bill grinnin keys with
stuff in old french and english
bill just underneath…

…on the way to the cleve
lands and the bloom fields
(this then the end of long
division) poe has she has
been charmed by *please*
*buy an cat or dog food* for
what what kind of days
thinking of our spaniel *kitty*
*kitty kitty* helps you with 7
days a week helps you 55
days in pell-mell helps you
once upon a time (well do
you) if not pull if so part
then you will see the tall
thin ladies they are lookout
they are unfinished they
will make a comeback as
heart's desire (mainly were
whispering I am lost in this
book) and then the flood
came along which he liked
(it was my country cousin
caught up with curtis (doris)
doris in the dock-road mostly
aged 5 danced a queen strut
through the cluster block
to the lifting bridge its soffits
gently curved and there
danced a quarter-round with
the rough-&-toughs (uprights
of silos) where she sang the
one about pouring on water
for a barrel of pears…

…this is part two licking it
in the mixer-courts (this is
mini-milk this is calippo
this is twister) stopping here
here and here they fan out
for tessa who is lost in the
volute (she moves through
the fair & she moves through
the field or she was a runner
she was a strayer (password
*french entry* no this is not
a dance its a france like all
the others turn turn turn (we
often find them near the
finger-jetty di style (repeat
I've these counter-rounds
as are all ding-dong all day
long dinging the life and
work of bar tracery (strike
out for what I say of *him*
he was twice rolled in the
dirty hole in the morning
he was a tree a pretty picture
a dogtrot that he was a little
one that he was called a little
one (arrival whitish he says
he was from none-other &
then-away) & that it extends
in length by rapid jerkings
to and fro & that it pointed
upwards & that they fancy
that foxe gawdy & hatton
as twisted again…

…and the two cousins they
(his step with her step) her
ecstasy his side this she did
hose-in-hose the first to flower
my primrose (no they were
cowslips yes they were and
so on to earls and peers (see
those words see how as they
kiss they all fall down and
so on that a man's hair fall
off and took off her hat and
the only thing she laid her
head on the valley (in this
one it is plum in this one it is
cherry and apples (english
I'm english & what a thing
it was *spred the whole land*
I'll electrify I'll do plant &
a little green border (the list
of ground & pulled out a chub
(them tight their twilight like
side by side with my english
life (dam the dam with moss
what did the foxes & another
thing we will be yours (me &
my girl brainwashing belong
somewhere else ps elafonisi
been torn off (the waves (few
were at the table (threw glasses
(land of that ship & picked a
bastard oxlip & for-you-a-
saw-them-parley how now
the barley corn in rows…

…at the same time corinth
radiated braque and léger
but this suggests pictures
who have always allies
which is to say both dream
sweets and pigtails between
the black bits and the brown
bits (black left is a sell &
this has none poor little
open-and-shut things (steeple
people which was fingers
whizzing over glass (signed
*oats*) and bad results (signed
grape-eater) by way of the
blue in it (now in the blue
of it) daddy daddy now he
is a sponge (sensation of
being a sponge is I never
let go (signed *east* of the
heavenly organ is this the
first second or where the
sun rises (*if this* lift here &
bolt if this alas I am that
weary ah (all bee it a fig
a pet a mistress still & them
are beads lady & them
a white roses & the spoon
it stand straight up & blue
go all the way through
(that weren't pink that were
her head hurling a discus
that weren't a finial that
were the lightest brass…

…a thick gloom fell that the
year the summer windeed
froze me (said I to myself
must I change me must I to
chant songs and learn to
change me must I breathe
cold) and yet that the air
I was to chant a thed froze
(thed lear thed lear your
sullen hymns beneath the
cold dirges of the cold
dirges of the cold lear the
baffled year the baffled)
sullen hymns of the sun-
shine air and dirges of the
sullen hymns of the sullen
hymns yet triumphange
me (the air I change my-
self and sunshine and
summer was warm enough
yet that the air a thed froze
and dirges of thick gloom
fell the cold dirges of
defeath (yet triumphange
me) reel'd beneath your
sullen hymns of through
(yearn to chant songs said
I to myself must I must I
must I warm enough thed
lear the baffled through
the baffled (said I breath
me) your summer windeed
through the cold and dark…

…hello & everything this
voice is back (killed it off
as stated above that is rare
as red closet yellow closet
*bad boy loose woman mig-*
*rant worker* (they broke him
ope and hid in all his inlets
(the one according to mr owl-
head they were spoiled &
left at a b & c but he sound
like everyone else & he
sound like everyone else
(the usual two & two is fair
& from three a win-win &
then there were none (they
all gone pair-bonding called
also night life (please sir
permission to blaze & as
he does red clouds of sunset
in the west was painted on
his coat (this way he was
disguised as a spreading
display which won me a
fiver & her eyes flashed
(it's keepers booty miss)
& *a yellow patch to match*
with no patch he was all in
jags & numbers will tell you
how it was pulled out &
some-be-lies some-be-true
even this was found when
the end is known (one end
is nothing but mum…

…me me me towels them
these three nymphs sinks
off gavdos (orange fizz of
poem on water) nymphs
just as stony as completely
walks in & out (got nut
brown breasts) there in the
sea with you it does not go
back so simply olive boy
shake yr fishing tree kid a)
say calypso kid b) daphne
(is no kid c) no such nut
brown no helen trunks ps
peace is off  forgot its songs
(a couple mass murder me
the attacks was a lot of
children did it as shook all
its fruits off so *oligos* these
little fruits get mash up by
stormy love (see where they
step over the water mark)
where are blue sky at night
blue sky in the morning (can
it be the end (to be eyed
up by a mantis & moved
by a story of bending over
(he did he didn't pick it up
(*aman aman*) and you were
a filled candy slip o god
have come to her rock has
come to her 99 church fathers
let loose on her imprisoned
let loose…

*. . . from this famous house*
to the hôtel du cap in cap
(and I joined whispered
cowardice) consequently
what is common (butler
emergence) about time
time as that which filled
full of the sound of birds
as they all leaf the wood
as is no comfortable feel
for them these ring-a-ring-
a-purley-men each a one
thumber take it in & eat
me green & see very &
*verbum sap* that's natural
(underlet underlet) the land
as what was called ridge-
rhyme & so if it's simple
race me his shy discoverer
(one riding one rifling last
words *world* and *cloud* that
forms loops (new forms)
hence dittany it grow up
into a radish & tracey who
is unserious & glory glory
as two acid radicals which
anyone is in a class hence
dittany of crete from corner
to corner & into disuse
(the chaser run into his shadow
(the women in suffolk
(the badlings . . .

…this little tower went to
market and this is bliss v
bliss bliss was drunk and
this is little miss bliss and
story block (leaning flaps
ground berry rooming rm)
yes I'm looking for pops
& that was phia my mother
(dred yards mended hotels
handled metres) what world
is in pieces I dont know its
as old as car car car and
which no one reads this
is despair and dont fit (story
block) leaning ground end
of the line this is not the dor
hath not the lexicon for elf-
lock or rosalie rosalie is one
of two persons who *togidere*
*is a coomb of hony* is for
silver is for gold which let
out water than silver & gold
& story block (this old tower
came rolling rolling down
(flings ellipsis (false lips in
the house of love in which
case spelt *door* and so on
where the valleys end and
the hills begin they are to
marry and (we call them
glides like something left
before the pause (like bliss
an unexploded final stop…

## vol 3

"Sequences are bad when they are the wrong sequences."

*Christopher Alexander, The Timeless Way of Building*

…and without a stretcher
but we must stay happy etc
etc continuous & happy (but
I had not been talking robs
or step fits but it can do not
to understand say say when
misled or not to understand
*happy hugs* and that you can
never tell that you can not-lose
if you (so to speak) in your
home raise empty hands (yes
the ladder the peeping how)
things are outside (they were
all bound (related) some from
dent classes or some dent class
of their own (nate anything is
abandoned & let alone & all
is clear & so on from an
abandoned area (places the old
let alone do *not* know they are
reversed they are replaced by
are daily bread and broken as
to say parks the pioneer may
still go out and parks the pioneer
filling himself and did give way
his two legs in the spring there
while the world was so wide &
out into the sunshine & what
remains is rips (fill it up you
mr this is a sult maids house
(must overthrow must over
throw before us murder an
virgin or an venus…

…got get me a first time
as what she wants is what
it looks like how they think
I been with pairs & pairs
& shoved it with my sister
& the lines *wrong jungle*
& *get off the split* like
when I was in "springs"
& people thinking robert
hanson sweetly tosses her
(the irony the irony of
"springs" before a girl can
say *good girl* or *the dead*
*girls are having the best*
*time at the party* (they partied
with a ring with a frost &
with a ordinary thing (jones
is a ordinary thing (oh jones
the world will not stand it
no threads & losing it
after he drops away his
gear (oh tara suck up so
much rime she rime away
(the ground (this lamp
(the thing (& now we are
bored by this lamp as its
a serious ray (bobs *saucy*
*spray* withheld & found
later where it says "ready
to strike now" his shot
form pressed into the
round (nothing there but
man hours precious...

…most wanted the stars
of heaven looking down
on john james smith (john
james of a-only yard) he
& his classy otter breaking
through the day mayor blister
and his five times table once
times five is a billion pressed
again *the early curlew is a
savage* (turn again john james
smith suited for large who
saw him alias "hot summers
day" between 7 & 7 take the
risk himself alias jan alias
d & e he is known not to
hand over the money (once
john james smith was bathing
in honey (see him go with a
slim otter (fiddler freed (see
his figures 12 38 12 "he is
growing into the perfect
creature of may" one case
goes (2 fives 0800 555 111
and that the figure will rise
prolific smith rose tree of
the first state who does get
clean away in silent night
"one of them bathing in
honey" hid in a fleecy trail
& the result is some poise
(3 fives misunderstood as
not here as turning again
into one of these…

...*I'm still numb* from
a tattoo of the chin say
m carroll his thrill fishin'
near a lake it happen
my win with 19 19 4 19
9.7 250 my lucky break
my lucky break 2 months
in a -late factory spend
spend spendin' & one in
sir e john (tear away
m carroll he was lost
count of when he was
on xmas day when he was
the biggest ever swiggin'
on a empty lanson at
the institute of winnin'
*I'm still numb* say his
lucky dip (his lucky dip
is sandra the chinese for
steve & I will not come
off with sir e john for
he is a sinny man &
is powered by primus
yeah he is a onanist he
is so happy in the -late
factory with his life out
like any thrill say m carroll
so far who is in the game
*I'm still numb* near a lake
he said I was like when
he was 10 he said on
xmas day on xmas day
(& couldn't help but cry...

...life should be *this isn't*
*you* and its yours a day
out and a day out with
accounts (how much they
save (what ever she brings
I said just living say they
save everything every
week in pictures by *great*
*bikini survey* by *captain*
*says he* by *pc hello boys*
it does give you a family
trip & these are still free
(barclay bank (loyd bank
(hbc which stand in relation
to no one (o praise this
town which is so sure of
my lean boy & let us mind
the flashes last the sea
don't look like this no
more now I'm inserted
(you were served by merly
(you were served by luba
(my lean boy is gaining &
hopes his filly will stay
something like this (all
my hearers shh you can
rave long on these how
we are all pillin' on mdf
(ssh these are my own
mini days and nights
pocket dead spend the
rest holding them up then
live without breathing...

…go litel guns of april yr
pop pop for grief (repeat
the queen is not dead long
live zombie closedown)
long live the arch long
live our stiff sons & all
yr shiny cunts long live
the young sailors stick it
in every night for the *r r p*
all over pink and stepping
on it with their wonderful
life of lights out (sleepy
head we salute you and
your fierce boys which
buried the wren which is
a common stutterer and
nothin but a tweeny which
got caught up in a bush
singing *one of the f-family*
& what if you could see
this in your house & what
& then what *as being nearer*
as *the sun setting* in that
*the cold in it* (one person
and another there there
under the stair one by one
dropping or marching or
even stalking like a long
legged bird which is in the
field (or between standing
& stamping it does drop &
rushes in with bricks &
stones…

…thats all from the land
of red-top let go let go
we wont forget commander
M (lyric poet) (the sailors
bore him) doing easter &
going in live (I'm off) & left
his remains with baby friends
just by holding them this
drippy day give us are arms
as we are from very far &
led by others which is
stripped herrings (the image
of them says come & hang
me again & its so obvious
her dogs are swapping her
& jarring it to go (we are
there & its broken but they
are good & they dance in
the sun & thats her boy
boiling perfectly into a
nation (we had gone so far
and your just in england &
it was nothing but hens &
a blonde in blue kept us all
in arcady or everyone into
my dull lap (its a love story
of trick hymns who meet &
make up and so on in england
*& there & then & there & then*
& her boy between but come
away & slimmer just by
holding it (buy either & you
can go behind the dresser…

...something beginning w/
(down bert) the cheaper
the sofa the (down bert)
her hands on a dish her
right hand a final *so cold
in the frigidaire (33 is
pretty* but her stances thin
& pretty as a found bell
as a small click (easy chair)
& the yellow sidewalks
goofassing in the wee hours
constantly killed granite
a way-turned light marked
"lockers" file rapists rising
a cop coming "combination
sweaters" the *latticini* in c
(reaching de witt he turned
off the gas (down bert) is it
a nose or a hose what ship
are you *on* (landing those
hands & our bringing girls
of knotty pine (thats good
because you are a dull
mugger now in a slow arc
(seriously I really *am*
mugging again up to the
curb *ing ting cinct* wildly
now (if I was a badly
framed mugger thats all)
and then he said nylons
gone forever ping-cats what
cats ping-cats ever cracked
you must be bert she said...

...besides poetry he flops
over on us (poetry nak) w/
my eye my little dam fuck
protest ok rexroth many
many thanks I just left so
much for li'l' ol' bones
no one prints 'em
slacknesses fit that single
gross poster (also that I
am very attracted to the
maintains which is fucking
dull it says nothing about
isabelle et marie as gin
relations says ann to him
(you spot *carbona* that
allusion to stout wires in
piles just so so taken is ply
ie me ie poor e ie fuck 'em
through these poems (this
is just to say I rented it
off dec sliding south-east
(how the docks like bon
voyage like in little dam
boats to london makes the
gig hideous just sliding into
such strips as flatness
bareness dam married chair
kicking is the bug (fuck that
phrase *honest content*
o to o to be o to be old
mans organs in aluminum
lakes of d & c...

...into the rock face
love byron to someone
(halt einer meiner are
innocent or see its mined
with carols dog (the dog
races the name of the
dog is the theory that
simon & garfunkel are
moths (french ones e.g.
monly positions e.g. stilts
e.g. silikon und kohle
close up like I need a
fucking neon family (no
I love byron & the band
suede & wank over throb
evans & I go in a corn
field very happy yes yes
like because it was funny
we had ning drinks we
had tabus fun we had
crete without crete &
me going to top spot
(lean on it & er it was
up again dancing through
the kings cross (the
story so far some of it
was tiny snap shots
some is a description
& some is sort of gathered
to make things flash yes
yes & then I make a retired
canadian couple I mean
you just spotted it...

...into the rock face
love byron to someone
& the poem hangs out
in the same way as the
monarch (circling bristling
chuckling) only a fool
would say *all the way*
elizabeth the second as
names are a hundred
hundred identical names
for appearance and ease
(special guest monarchs
& wars of the nineteenth
century & wars of the
twentieth century may
well begin with wars of
the twentieth century
(result (the wars of the
finches the wars of the
finches yacht & piler n
has tried to quit even
this small advance (em
dash dash cram it all in
to made four errors four
hundred errors of the
wars of the rosses and
monarchs and the like
they serve as a.) cause
b.) result of wars of the
rosses (never end a line
with a dollar sign bracket
parenthesis bracket periods
complete sentences...

...this spelling is ok 'tex'
run along over the place
'tex' the word here is ok
it is ok that have already
been painted instead of
the house (the painter is
empty and dry instead
of painting and stroke
stroke filling each view
with a pencil top (I leave
this painter something
which mean the *e t* tapes
where the ambiguity is
high wide and long and
not perfect (you may
leave the rin place 'tex'
you may run into the
other house where all
along the other 2 are all
over filling each other
with lime using lime to
instead of filling each
other with number one
(the word here is the
same is that this spelling
is as to the first painter
which make the following
ok to the ultra painter the
one where where all the
letters are in one inch
lines one in yellow one
in colour (this is 'ok' tex
this is 'ok'...

...& went & grabbed
pylons (scrap ones) aucun
wind aucun swell surfers
restless dipping moving
in the port of dramont &
this raid failed because
of our small mansion at
the edge of unnevenness
(fragments of the wrecks
scrap everywhere a small
tip truck lost in its thick
sheets no one knows where
is jean suzon where is the
dun diver (as if the fifties
(rounded broken) can't
locate the english (on
the right on the right the
surfers dipping moving
their custom of exploding
on the coast their pheno-
menon of shift (nobody is
not never found (a true
dive before nature grows
hot the sunset of the sun
on the heaps of the next
thing to be seen (pylons
clamped on) the airport
in principal fragments
its any thing in the way
a cornish door a stem (no
it ain't green its purple
from the purple for dock
from the purple for rock...

...as this is a story of
what I did to begin w/
the viaduc is not for
pod boy its for conrad
conrad was a smudge
& pushed me in a oil
tanker with no lid (q.)
whats a lid for its for
a.) its for a daisy & a.)
its for a chain ie a chain
gang which march in
lines to the sea which
is for passing water to
the equator (they hit on
this till it is a ditch &
send it to france like
that dry gash of mine I
got for falling in a oil
tanker with the lip on
(q.) whats a lip for its
for a.) its for a fish &
a.) its for a monk ie a
monk gang boiled to
gether for glue (I never
heard of that on my
holiday but I heard of
a pound of spots &
a tree with a snatch
& a white gal turn into
a pea (they who lie up
river & grow rare by
spelling v v v v v...

...dear sir there were
these 3 dots which could
sing one did not say he
was free one did not say
a bar and a dog which
carry its shit by as a hobby
was made up of three dots
in a line (the difference in
a line and a dot is a line
is not shit & did not invent
sue lawley (ha ha the ur
sonata) I am in love with
steak and am a genius dot
dot dot (no thats called a
hinge as in dear sir there
were these three lines
which never said a word
first was a a-line which is
the wrong shape & first
was a b-line wet with drops
first was a c-line a sounding
line & first was etc etc &
all these are the same line
(the difference in a line &
a hinge is a hinge is where
it swaps sue lawley for
*o thou bride smell* & *o*
*could I but launder this*
*fishy* & the lights go down
on her dog which is also
a hinge (trot trot trot) in
other words this goes on
in parks everywhere...

...you cannot rave long
on a mound so say any
when they mix it with
the yabsley boys (this
from my back head they
were only in the urbs
for a clavier from von
roar like this-'n'-that w/
a handslicer (better a
handstander than a god
house (this little book
was just grouped into
his favourite cranes
falling down on the falling
falling sherbert girls
my daughters out flat
in the shealing if she say
I am not 13 & lute-pure
in the halting-place that
woman has got thee
harried the harps have
queerd me into a blanc-
mange ('sgraffito from
the time of caxton goes
like the tap cock late a
piece of up a stem a stem
the housemaids shakes
so send down mildew
(dryden watching from
the *maritima* hair-rich
rings at the raving at the
knocking-on (a rickety
thing (one speaker (wild...

*...mounde life on the upp*
his xmas singles is early
& late & everywhere out
of true decking (true or
false the land of essexe
is mainly painted on the
inside true or false inside
there is no such place as
true or false I believe in
the very bells of england I
believe they was then dead
mens bells down among
the still hangings of winter
I believe in a field of sticks
in diss where clare the
jenny-rider swings again
I believe in most of queens
since I left essexe (no this
is not about lee or philip
or jack or paul who fall
under other regions not yet
clear (ports & rotten ports
his sucked dog will change
its name to south london
mix and essexe can-celled
again & I believe in lids
mind my names lid & pin
& often I am up to it in
the home garden & in with
yr fingers & meets him
inna worm bin (not yet) &
meets him inna lily pad its
true his nails describes it...

...cone falls in the wood
and he dies of joined up
shyness (thats harry he
presses so hard he makes
holes in school *vous aime
le cinema harry non jaime
la musique* "pop" (this
shows the loop of the de-
scender each action she
performs like she went on
mining (ask *is it soft* or
such as *is it red* when you
wash his dirty toys & as I
cross the rode he just
grab me in his boot & as
he cross me out I just
shine up my very bud in
the rolls & curls & let him
have a day out in my mouth
saying "horsie" or "no"
or *vous aime le greve* &
he digs so hard he makes
holes in her heart but she
and he are only cut out for
the day & are stacked up
by the butcher & the baker
they pull in with 'em mixing
& meeting & in charge of
lights on & when it comes
off of her lousy reflectors
they flash on the front seat
and pass around the sun
dial so yellow it hurts...

…I (binger) with my din
friends in the fields open
up my kit off & I wager
in the foundry your bell
counts over did you fuck
off in the inn did you sing
it to a birdy did you see
this did you see this (daisy
lane first where he thrilled
me later my legs in his mouth
& how he wore me in the
shallow end (the alley then
ringing with his light new
stripes he collapses all over
going I am not your failed
high street I am your water
scene (there is one scene
by an eel brook where we
filled him in there by the
eel brook (in the inn are of
no use to anyone in the fields)
& again & again in with it
til we lie down in the lane
with the ringing (so the bells
of bell alley) & he all open
going r i p you are always
be a r i p & the birdy singing
*coo coo* or *tac tac tac* or
sometimes a little bit of a call
(hop hop) (hop hop) (hop
hop) & if it is over it is in
london & if it is more in the
day it is all over…

…moving across the
ground in the summer
so rev rev he goes these
are only my bike notes
my only bike notes &
& it all floats up but
is not heard in england
it is not on my radio which
also tells me I am for it
my radio which makes this
noise (my other radio is
like chains (this is what
my radio tells me get it
from smiths who have it
in for you (*crcrcrcrcrcrc*)
the interferers come in
(*crcrcrcrcrcrc*) they
move around like sally
(*crcrcrcrcrcrc*) language
english I live in a trough
in the uk and I am fed
nuts (in the winter I also
use sound (*crcrcrcrcrc*)
shorter sound to get nuts
I am very handsome after
on saturday I will get up
see the join jane sees it
she is not like the other
months (I mean seasons)
she is a crack fairy at
the treatment bar & after
outside jobs she leaves
us all her fairy stains…

…in all directions her
snakes colour but she
doesn't sing about it her
negro army any more
which would tune into
all of them sailing to the
black island on a cling
film & found it again
the shallow end only the
densest end to get off
but who wants to live
in it as a crowd and as
a foam cloud moving
moving coastal packets
with their kind of music
love evolving in wind
wrecks which is where
they have arrived and
they don't believe it any
more than she does her
lungs like at flood the
blood ticking sound and
she wild on such points
as the portant business
the correct thing partly
dome partly by the tide
neatly and reached for
being tied for like to a
sound-valuable between
the same rubbed source
(what tin or ruff what
cart she gives out such
damn small commands…

# Why I wrote stretchers

*"I live on the island where people shout 'It is they!' at the voyagers as though they knew of their coming and feared them."*

This epigraph at the beginning of the first set of stretchers is from *The Voyage of Maelduin*, an 11th century Irish poem selections of which I first came across in a copy of the magazine Eleventh Finger. Maelduin, discovering that his father has been killed by brigands, builds a boat and sails with his foster-brothers to avenge him. On their voyage they visit a number of Fabulous Islands, which include the following:

> An island of enormous Ants, each as large as a foal.
>
> An island of Great Birds.
>
> An island where the sea hurls salmon through a stone valve into a house.
>
> An island with a Wondrous Beast, which can turn its body round inside its skin and revolve its skin round its body.
>
> An island of shouting birds.
>
> The island of laughter. The last of Maelduin's foster-brothers lands, laughs with the multitude there and has to be abandoned.

I started writing stretchers when I lived on the Isle of Dogs, which at the time I figured as one of these fabulous islands.

*Stretchers* began partly as a response to Chapter 1 of *Lights Out for the Territory* where the author Iain Sinclair quickly crosses what he calls "Dog island" dismissing it for its lack of graffiti because "there's no surface rough enough to take the pen." The Isle of Dogs – *faux*-isle as Sinclair notes – is home to many of the stretchers and I, an invader on the wave of the area's "redevelopment", house-sat there for over 15 years. I took offence at Sinclair's totalising attack on the isle's "smooth" Thatcherite credentials and began, petulantly, to think about all the mounds of dog shit there as a kind of interruptive writing which induced in the walker a state of constant paranoia: "for graffiti there's dogshit it's a kind/of writing can be scried an inventory/taken of say colour consistency" I wrote in the first stretcher. It's as simple as that. The word "swipe" occurs a number of times in *Lights Out for the Territory* though never the result of a white Reebok passing through one of these pliable deposits. The meeting of shoe and shit seems to me as good a way of thinking about the stink of transaction as some flat plastic moving through a PDQ machine. Both leave a permanent stain on the fetishized object. But I get beyond myself. "Trapped in an isthmus of signs, not language," Sinclair could have found a whole new language not only by reading the walls but also the pavements, pavements smeared by shit and cracked into Cobbing-esque pages by years of neglect and by truckloads of superslim soldiers feeding the area's 'regeneration.' O Brave New World that has such language in it!

Each stretcher is nominally a 33-line unit. The decision to use a 33-line form was ultimately banal, based on my age at the time of writing the first set of them, although one night I was sitting in the bar underneath Centre Point just off Tottenham Court Road when a French woman there asked me my age. When I told her, she told me to watch out because Jesus had died at 33. The 33-line form was thus also talismanic, though not all the poems are 33 lines long because sometimes I miscounted.

The poems incorporate a lot of found material. This material is much of it (though by no means all of it) verbal detritus heard or seen on journeys through this city. Much of it is also taken from books I had read or books that I would never have thought of reading. Pillaging cheap secondhand texts for material enforced another kind of reading which was partial, discontinuous and manic. Page 33 of texts became for a time a focus – Ed McBain's *The Mugger* or John Cowper Powys' *A Glastonbury Romance* for instance. There's some lovely stuff about primroses in this last. Other found material was more directed. A number of the stretchers were wholly lifted from a single source.

Each stretcher is initiated by a first line which is, I have realised, a ringing off of words from Artaud's famous letter of June 5, 1923, to Jacques Rivière where Artaud complains of his "terrifying malady of the spirit." I don't, I think, have this malady, but what interests me about Artaud in this letter is his registering the unknowable way in which thought becomes word and the sense of risk attendant on seizing that form and fixing it however imperfect it might be. The opening line of each stretcher "sounded" right to me though mostly they were those imperfect forms of which Artaud speaks. They "bothered" me as a "bewilderment of noise," a phrase turned over and over in my head. The writing down of the opening line momentarily stilled the noise, gave it some sort of clarity, though the necessity of deciding what to do immediately after getting it down made it impossible to dwell there for long. Was it Robert Creeley who told his students to get rid of the opening of poems because the poem only ever got going after that? The opening is treated then as little more than a discardable grace-note, no? Stretchers retain the ghostly excisions of the openings of Creeley's students' poems.

A prosodist once told me that my use of line endings is aberrant and that it ruins the stretchers. I agree, but would add that stretchers themselves *are* ruins, constructed ruins. I have tried whenever possible to avoid the "effects" which a line ending can produce. Any "effect" produced by a line ending is accidental. I do not see stretchers as having lines. They are more prose pieces with a frayed right margin. They are tatters, ragged flags.

The measure of stretchers is not the line it is the phrase. The phrase disregards the line or at least contests the line, threatens the line's existence. The right-hand limit of stretchers is a site of conflict, not between the end of the line and the "white space" of the page (not the margin or "margent" of older liminal analogies such as "sea and strand") but an internal struggle between two ways of thinking.

I have for a while now found myself looking at prose as if it consisted of lines. I have been drawn (no I am not the first) to the left-hand margin where the occasional word is broken across the turn of one (line) into the next. The hyphen, which itself has a quiet but interesting history, should nevertheless be abolished so that this breaking open of words remains unannounced. It gives you new whole words like "ning," "cinct" and "tabus." If stretchers have a procedure it's that they are assembled out of discrete semantic units, often very small ones. The process is one of reconstitution, sense packets emerging from putting together disparate elements. I'm not certain what the effect of this is except that when I read out what I've written it does all make sense.

And sometimes I do still use hyphens.

All spelling mistakes are deliberate.

Each stretcher tells a story and each story contains many other stories. The opening (line) of each stretcher is in a way another way of saying "once upon a time."

The opening is a measure for the rest of the stretcher, not necessarily in terms of content, but certainly in terms of (line) length. This is what gives stretchers their shape. If stretchers have a constraint it's that they can't be too wide. The need to stop them getting too wide has on occasions led to some interesting visual results. The first stretcher of volume 3 seems to have the front of a ship sailing out of it.

The title "stretchers" was, then, a response to their emerging form. Casting about for a title, there was also always the opening of Huckleberry Finn:

> You don't know about me without you have read a book by the name of *The Adventures of Tom Sawyer*; but that ain't no matter. That book was made by Mr. Mark Twain, and he told the truth, mainly. There was things which he stretched, but mainly he told the truth. That is nothing. I never seen anybody but lied one time or another, without it was

> Aunt Polly, or the widow, or maybe Mary. Aunt Polly – Tom's Aunt Polly, she is – and Mary, and the Widow Douglas is all told about in that book, which is mostly a true book, with some stretchers, as I said before.

*"As I said before."* The "I" here is Finn, Twain and Clemens, all three of them and none of them, and the narrator is both within and "without" the narrative. The first "stretcher" in Huckleberry Finn is its opening sentence, with its *faux-naïf* use of the folk idiom ("without" for "unless"), the disingenuous rubbishing by Twain of his own earlier book (*The Adventures of Tom Sawyer* as "no matter") and its levels of narratorial fictiveness set up in deliberately phoney opposition to a supposedly stable and solid reader identified as "You." How the reader feels proud to be the first word of this book! This is of course the ultimate confidence trick, giving the victim or "mark" (and mark that word here) the illusion that s/he is the one in control when from the start s/he is already being taken in, in this case by the author. We are "taken in" here not only by having a spell cast over us, by being woven into the fabric of the narrative and letting ourselves be spellbound by Twain's prose, but also by being absorbed by the author and given his name too – we as readers become "Mark(s)." To quote from later on in the book, where Huck is talking about how he prefers stews (or "a barrel of odds and ends" as he calls them) to individually cooked items: "things get mixed up, and the juice kind of swaps around, and the things go better."

Stretchers then as a barrel of odds and ends, or a glory hole.

Stretchers seemed to be a good title for my

pieces. I love the naïve language Twain gives Huck to use as it has no place in the world, no home. Or at least if it does it's a very fragile one, like his and Jim's raft. It lives in the gaps of the languages used by grown ups and professionals who use smooth, specialised languages which say "keep out." These specialised languages are more often than not allied to specialised practices which solidify into accepted practices, practices which obscure possible alternatives as well as obscuring actual histories and deliberately sabotaging alternatives. These "official" languages need to be broken into by poets and deliberately misused as much as possible. One stretcher in the second set sources the London Docklands edition of Nikolas Pevsner's *Buildings of England* for some architectural terminology. Take the compound "queen-strut", not a dance but a piece of wood which sticks up out of a beam in a roof, out of a tie-beam, and attaches to a collar lying under the purlin which is sunk into the principal rafter. You would have a problem if you tried to build a building with a dance but it's very useful to have a dance in the building of a stretcher. Imagine such a building anyway. At least you couldn't work in it.

Stretchers also as a pack of lies.

I would like all the stretchers to be read out loud on the radio by a tag team of pre-school children.

*Jeff Hilson*

*A longer version of this was published as* The Radiator *3, November 2005.*

OTHER TITLES IN PRINT FROM REALITY STREET EDITIONS:

*POETRY SERIES*
Kelvin Corcoran: *Lyric Lyric*
Maggie O'Sullivan: *In the House of the Shaman*
Susan Gevirtz: *Taken Place*
Allen Fisher: *Dispossession and Cure*
Denise Riley: *Mop Mop Georgette*
Fanny Howe: *O'Clock*
Maggie O'Sullivan (ed.): *Out of Everywhere*
Cris Cheek/Sianed Jones: *Songs From Navigation* (+ audio CD)
Nicole Brossard: *Typhon Dru*
Lisa Robertson: *Debbie: an Epic*
Maurice Scully: *Steps*
Barbara Guest: *If So, Tell Me*
Tony Lopez: *Data Shadow*
Denise Riley: *Selected Poems*
Anselm Hollo (ed. & tr.): *Five From Finland*
Lisa Robertson: *The Weather*
Robert Sheppard: *The Lores*
Lawrence Upton: *Wire Sculptures*
Ken Edwards: *eight + six*
Peter Riley: *Excavations*
David Miller: *Spiritual Letters (I-II)*
Allen Fisher: *Place*
Redell Olsen: *Secure Portable Space*
Tony Baker: *In Transit*
Maurice Scully: *Sonata*

*4PACKS SERIES*
1: *Sleight of Foot* (M Champion, H Kidd, H Tarlo, S Thurston)
2: *Vital Movement* (A Brown, J Chalmers, M Higgins, I Lightman)
3: *New Tonal Language* (P Farrell, S Matthews, S Perril, K Sutherland)
4: *Renga+* (G Barker, E James/P Manson, C Kennedy)

*NARRATIVE SERIES*
Ken Edwards: *Futures*
John Hall: *Apricot Pages*
David Miller: *The Dorothy and Benno Stories*
Douglas Oliver: *Whisper 'Louise'*

Go to **www.realitystreet.co.uk**, email **info@realitystreet.co.uk** or write to the address on the reverse of the title page for updates.

Become a Reality Street Supporter!

Since 1998, more than 70 individuals and organisations have helped Reality Street Editions by being Reality Street Supporters. Those signed up to the current Supporter scheme, which runs till the end of 2006, are listed below (the list is correct at the time of going to press).

The Supporter scheme is an important way to keep Reality Street's programme of adventurous writing alive. As a Supporter, you receive all the press's titles free for three years. For more information, go to **www.realitystreet.co.uk** and click on the "About us" tab, or email **info@realitystreet.co.uk**

Peter Barry
Charles Bernstein
Clive Bush
Richard Cacchione
CCCP
Adrian Clarke
Mark Dickinson
Michael Finnissy
Allen Fisher/Spanner
Sarah Gall
Chris Goode
John Hall
Alan Halsey
Robert Hampson
Peter Hodgkiss
Fanny Howe
Harry Gilonis & Elizabeth James
Lisa Kiew
Peter Larkin
Tony Lopez
Ian McMillan
Richard Makin
Jules Mann
Mark Mendoza
Peter Middleton
Geraldine Monk
Maggie O'Sullivan
Marjorie Perloff
Pete & Lyn
Peter Philpott
Tom Quale
Peter Quartermain
Ian Robinson
Will Rowe
Susan Schultz
Maurice Scully
Robert Sheppard
John Shreffler
Peterjon & Yasmin Skelt
Hazel Smith
Valerie & Geoffrey Soar
Tony Trehy
Keith Tuma
Sam Ward
John Welch/The Many Press
John Wilkinson
Tim Woods
The Word Hoard
+ 8 anonymous